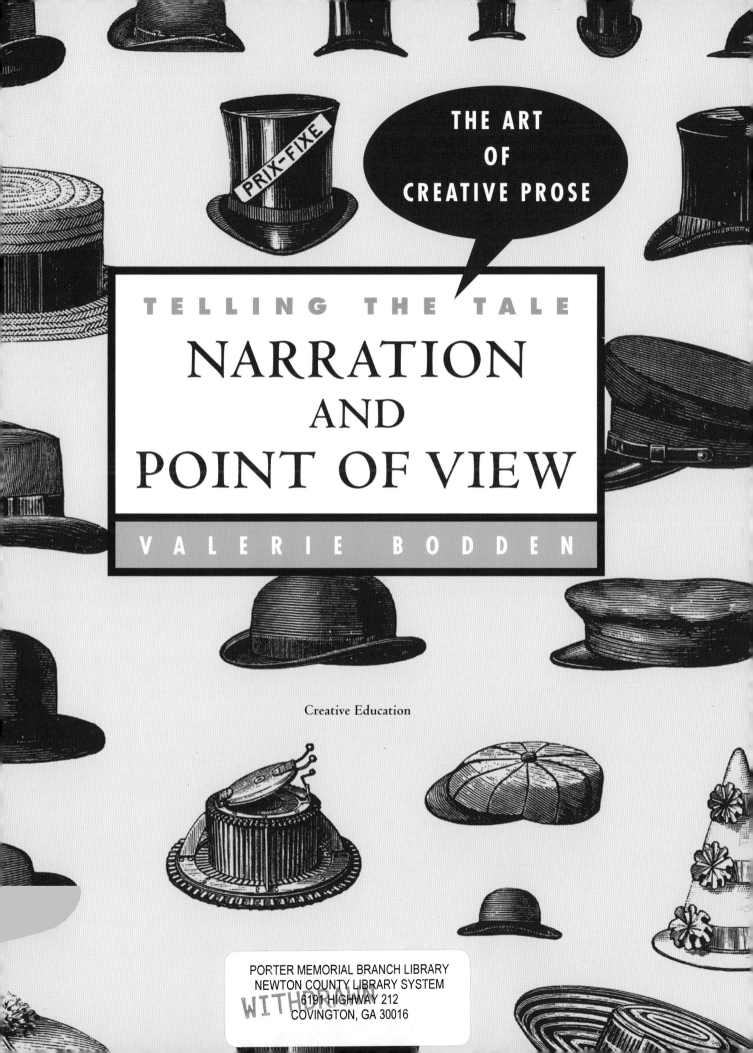

PRIX-FIXE

THE ART
OF
CREATIVE PROSE

TELLING THE TALE

NARRATION
AND
POINT OF VIEW

VALERIE BODDEN

Creative Education

Published by Creative Education
P.O. Box 227, Mankato, Minnesota 56002
Creative Education is an imprint of The Creative Company

Design and production by Stephanie Blumenthal
Art direction by Rita Marshall
Printed in the United States of America

Photographs by Alamy (Jack Carey, Mary Evans Picture Library, PARIS PIERCE), Getty
Images (Downey/W. and D. Downey, Michael & Patricia Fogden, Hulton Archive, Philippe
Marchand, Hans Neleman, Arthur Tress, Grey Villet/Time Life Pictures), Irving Zucker

Paragraphs on pages 30–33 (presenting the Price sisters' points of view) from pp. 22,
24, 25, 35 from *The Poisonwood Bible* by Barbara Kingsolver. Copyright © 1998 by
Barbara Kingsolver. Reprinted by permission of HarperCollins Publishers.

Library of Congress Cataloging-in-Publication Data

Bodden, Valerie.
Telling the tale: narration and point of view / by Valerie Bodden.
p. cm. — (The art of creative prose)
Includes index.
ISBN 978-1-58341-624-2
1. Fiction—Technique. 2. Narration (Rhetoric).
3. Point of view (Literature). I. Title. II. Series.

PN3383.N35B63 2008
808.3—dc22   2007004198

24689753

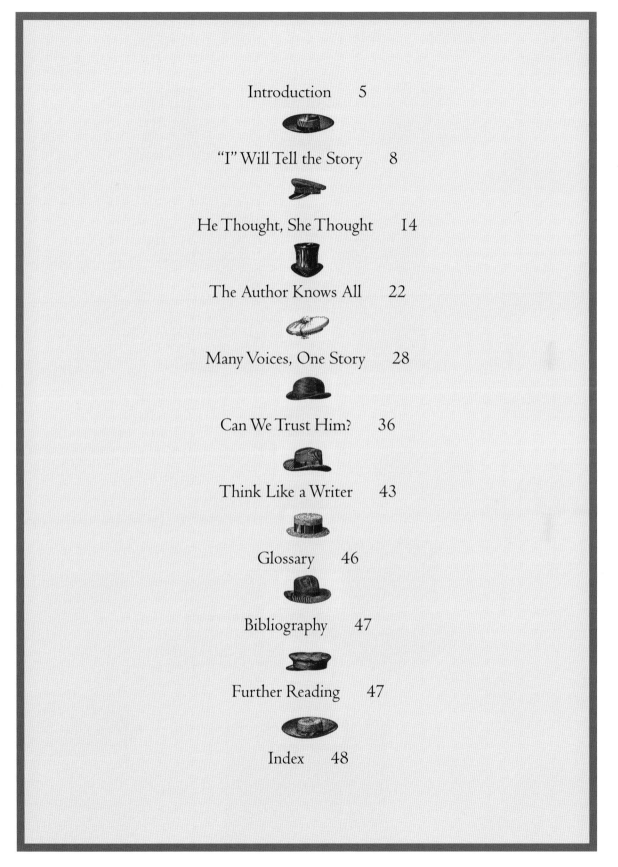

"DID I EVER TELL YOU ABOUT THE TIME I...?"

"Can you believe that she...?" "Did you hear that he...?" And so begins another story, part of the daily stream of anecdotes that falls upon our ears. Perhaps the abundance of true stories in our lives is why so many of us enjoy reading creative **prose**—short stories or novels. This form of writing lets us step into made-up lives and experience **fictional** characters' exciting, embarrassing, or entertaining moments. It leads us to connect with, laugh at, or detest these characters, in whom we can often see something of ourselves and our own lives.

Of course, in order for there to be a story at all, there must be a storyteller. In creative prose, that storyteller is called the narrator, and in almost every case, the choice of narrator is essential to the reader's understanding of a story, for no two narrators will ever tell the same story in the same way. The details and events they include, their descriptions of other characters, and even how they interpret the main action of the story will vary greatly among different narrators. In the case of a burglary, for example, you would hear three very different stories if you were told about it from the viewpoint of the victim, the burglar, and an objective bystander.

The narrator of a work of fiction can be the person who experienced the story—the protagonist, or main character—but it doesn't have to be. A secondary character, or even the author, can also serve as the narrator. Just as stories can have different narrators with different degrees of involvement in the story, those narrators can be presented from different points of view—usually **first person** ("I") or **third person** ("he" or "she")—which can further affect how readers experience the story, making them feel close to and sympathetic toward, or distant from and judgmental of, the narrator. With the use of the right point of view, a story can come alive, leading the reader to see the narrator almost like a real-life friend—or enemy.

"I" WILL TELL THE STORY

To the beginning writer of creative prose, it may seem that the easiest and most logical way to tell a story is from the first-person point of view, in which the narrator refers to himself as "I." After all, most people have plenty of experience in telling stories about themselves. This point of view is surprisingly difficult to work with, however. As an author writing a first-person narrative, you must remember that although you are using the word "I," you are not the narrator. Instead, you are creating a character from whose head you are thinking. That character may be a lot like you—or he may be completely different. Either way, everything you write must be from that character's **perspective**—and only from that perspective. The personality of the narrator should come through not only in his actions but also in his word choice—would he call a dress "blue," "cerulean," or not notice the dress at all? Does he see his chatty neighbor as "friendly," "lonely," or "nosy"? How he describes his life and the people in it can tell readers a lot about the kind of person he is.

One of the great advantages of the first-person story is that it puts readers inside the narrator's head, helping them to experience who the narrator is—his thoughts, feelings, and attitudes. They can see why he does what he does, which can help them to feel closer to the narrator and identify with him. We can see how a first-person narrative can help create a unique, sympathetic character in American author Mark Twain's novel *The Adventures of Huckleberry Finn* (1885), in which young Huck, the narrator, is rafting down the Mississippi River with Jim, an escaped slave.

Mark Twain (1835–1910)

This second night we run between seven and eight hours, with a current that was making over four mile an hour. We catched fish, and talked, and we took a swim now and then to keep off sleepiness. It was kind of solemn, drifting down the big still river, laying on our backs looking up at the stars, and we didn't ever feel like talking loud, and it warn't often that we laughed, only a little kind of a low chuckle....

Every night we passed towns, some of them away up on black hillsides, nothing, but just a shiny bed of lights, not a house could you see. The fifth night we passed St. Louis, and it was like the whole world lit up. In St. Petersburg they used to say there was twenty or thirty thousand people in St. Louis, but I never believed it till I see that wonderful spread of lights at two o'clock that still night. There warn't a sound there; everybody was asleep....

Mornings, before daylight, I slipped into corn fields and borrowed a watermelon, or a mushmelon, or a punkin, or some new corn, or things of that kind. Pap always said it warn't no harm to borrow things, if you was meaning to pay them back, sometime; but the widow said it warn't anything but a soft name for stealing, and no decent body would do it. Jim said he reckoned the widow was partly right and pap was partly right; so the best way would be for us to pick out two or three things from the list and say we wouldn't borrow them any more—then he reckoned it wouldn't be no harm to borrow the others.... Towards daylight we got it all settled satisfactory, and concluded to drop crabapples and p'simmons. We warn't feeling just right, before that, but it was all comfortable now. I was glad the way it come out, too, because crabapples ain't ever good, and the p'simmons wouldn't be ripe for two or three months yet.

11

From just this short excerpt, we learn a lot about Huck—without his ever coming out and telling us anything about himself directly. We can tell that he is uneducated (saying "catched" instead of "caught") but not unintelligent, as he is able to judge the speed of the river. We know that he hasn't yet seen much of the world and that he is working out his own system of rules about "borrowing" and stealing. Had Huck's character been related in the third person, using "he," we might have been more apt to judge his stealing, but because we can see how he has come to his conclusion about "borrowing," we are more likely to understand—though not necessarily agree with—his reasoning. In the third person, we also would likely have heard more of the author's voice and less of Huck's, making it harder for us to get a feel for his true character.

Although the first-person narrator can be extremely successful, as in the case of Huck Finn, there are times when a first-person narrator may hinder the story. First person may not be the best choice if the narrator has to relate how he performed a great, heroic act. Unless the narrator doesn't realize that the act was heroic, he won't be able to tell about it without sounding boastful—and likely **alienating** readers in the process. An alternative to having the **protagonist** relate his own heroism is to have a **peripheral** character who witnessed the protagonist's heroism serve as the narrator.

Another drawback of the first-person narrative is that the narrator can tell only about **scenes** he experienced or was told about, and cannot know the thoughts and feelings of other characters. If there's no way for the narrator to know about certain scenes, or if you need readers to know more than one character's thoughts with certainty, it's probably best to choose another point of view. For all of its challenges, though, a successful first-person story can be well worth the effort, leading readers to become closely connected with a story and its narrator. So pick up a piece of paper and try to create an "I" narrator that isn't you!

HE THOUGHT,

If talking about themselves seems natural to most people, talking about others probably seems almost as natural—if not more so. After all, it's much easier to tell a story about someone else's mistake or fear or lapse in judgment than your own. Perhaps that is why most fiction today is written in the third-person limited point of view, in which the author is technically the narrator but tells the story from the viewpoint of one character, referring to that character as "he" or "she." In this viewpoint, as in first person, readers are allowed to peer inside the head of this character and can see only those scenes at which she is present, but, unlike in a first-person narrative, the author of a third-person story can step out of the viewpoint character's head from time to time.

Although the third-person limited point of view may cause readers to lose some sympathy for the viewpoint character because they are not constantly in her thoughts as they are in a first-person narrative, it can also add another dimension to the story. The author can provide information that a first-person narrator would never tell us—information about the character's background, what she looks like (it's very awkward to describe yourself), or even things that the character doesn't understand about herself.

Third-person limited gives the author the freedom to write in his own **style**, although it is often a good idea to write at least the viewpoint character's thoughts in her own voice so that readers will know which ideas are the character's thoughts and which are the author's **exposition**.

SHE THOUGHT

As you read the following excerpt from the short story "An Occurrence at Owl Creek Bridge" (1890) by American author Ambrose Bierce, try to pick out which ideas are the author's and which belong to Peyton Farquhar, the viewpoint character, who is about to be hanged during the Civil War.

A man stood upon a railroad bridge in northern Alabama, looking down into the swift water twenty feet below. The man's hands were behind his back, the wrists bound with a cord. A rope closely encircled his neck. It was attached to a stout cross-timber above his head and the slack fell to the level of his knees. Some loose boards laid upon the sleepers [ties] supporting the metals of the railway supplied a footing for him and his executioners—two private soldiers of the Federal army, directed by a sergeant, who in civil life may have been a deputy sheriff....

The man who was engaged in being hanged was apparently about thirty-five years of age.... He wore a mustache and pointed beard, but no whiskers; his eyes were large and dark gray, and had a kindly expression which one would hardly have expected in one whose neck was in the hemp....

He closed his eyes in order to fix his last thoughts upon his wife and children. The water, touched to gold by the early sun, the brooding mists under the banks at some distance down the stream, the fort, the soldiers, the piece of drift—all had distracted him. And now he became conscious of a new disturbance. Striking through the thought of his dear ones was a sound which he could neither ignore nor understand, a sharp, distinct, metallic percussion like the stroke of a blacksmith's hammer upon the anvil; it had the same ringing quality. He wondered what it was, and whether immeasurably distant or near by—it seemed both. Its recurrence was regular, but as slow as the tolling of a death knell. He awaited each stroke with impatience and—he knew not why—apprehension. The intervals of silence grew progressively longer; the delays became maddening. With their greater infrequency the sounds increased in strength and sharpness. They hurt his ear like the thrust of a knife; he feared he would shriek. What he heard was the ticking of his watch.

Throughout this excerpt, we are shown both what is happening inside Peyton Farquhar's head and what is happening in the world outside of himself. As the story opens, we are looking at the scene of Peyton and the soldiers on the bridge from a distance. Then, Bierce brings us in closer, showing us what Peyton looks like. Soon, we are inside Peyton's head, hearing a maddening pounding but not knowing what it is. Then, the author steps in again, pulling us out of Peyton's thoughts to let us know that the "death knell" he hears is his own watch.

How might this story have been different if it were written from the first-person point of view? To begin with, the scene likely would have been much narrower, as the condemned Peyton, awaiting his hanging, wouldn't have paid attention to everything that was happening around him, nor would it have been logical for him to describe himself (and he certainly couldn't have seen the "kindly expression" in his own eyes). Because Bierce so successfully brings us into Peyton's head, we can feel almost as sympathetic toward him as if he had told us the story himself—maybe even more so, since after the section excerpted above, Bierce takes us back in time to show us the events that led to Peyton's hanging, something Peyton himself probably wouldn't have done as he spent his last moments of life trying to focus on his family.

Ambrose Bierce (1842–1914)

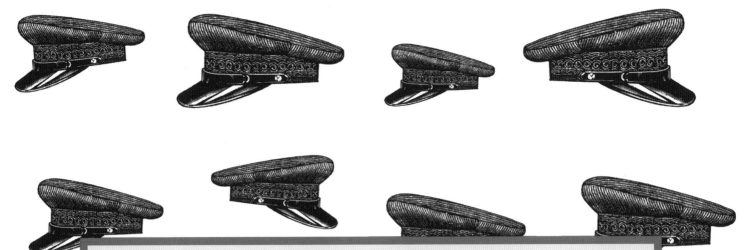

At the end of the story, Bierce effectively brings us into Peyton's head for an extended period, leading us to believe that he has escaped. The story ends as the narrator once again intervenes, stating that Peyton is dead, hanging by his neck from the bridge, and we suddenly realize that the whole escape scene was a hallucination. That's one of the great advantages of third-person limited—you can use it to effectively build suspense and surprise by entering and leaving the viewpoint character's mind at just the right moment.

Try it: you just might surprise yourself—and your readers!

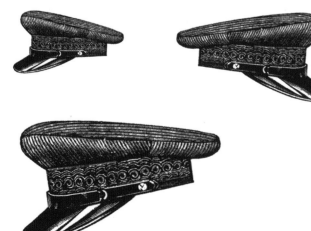

Most authors of fiction try to get readers to "suspend their disbelief"—that is, to be willing to believe that what they are reading is real, even though they know that it is simply a story, the creation of another's imagination. Some authors who write in the third-person **omniscient** point of view, however, constantly remind readers that what they are reading is a made-up tale—and that they are the ones who have made it up. Omniscient narrators know everything. They can enter the heads of any of their characters at any time, can relate information that no character knows, and can even insert their own thoughts about completely unrelated topics into the story. In fact, one of the hallmarks of 18th- and 19th-century omniscient literature was the interruption of the author (often called "authorial intrusion") to remark on the events of the story, ethics and morality in general, or his or her own worldview.

In the following excerpt from the novel *The History of Tom Jones, a Foundling* (1749), English writer Henry Fielding reveals the thoughts of both Mr. Allworthy—who discovers an abandoned infant in his bed—and his servant Mrs. Deborah Wilkins, all the while reminding us that we are reading a story, not experiencing a real event. As you read, think about whether or not you like this form. Do you think you would like to read an entire novel written in this manner?

Henry Fielding (1707–1754)

[Mr. Allworthy] was preparing to step into bed, when, upon opening the clothes, to his great surprise he beheld an infant, wrapt up in some coarse linen, in a sweet and profound sleep, between his sheets. He stood some time lost in astonishment at this sight; but, as good-nature had always the ascendant in his mind, he soon began to be touched with sentiments of compassion for the little wretch before him. He then rang his bell, and ordered an elderly woman-servant to rise immediately, and come to him; and in the mean time was so eager in contemplating the beauty of innocence, appearing in those lively colours with which infancy and sleep always display it, that his thoughts were too much engaged to reflect that he was in his shirt when the matron came in. She had, indeed, given her master sufficient time to dress himself; for out of respect to him, and regard to decency, she had spent many minutes in adjusting her hair at the looking-glass, notwithstanding all the hurry in which she had been summoned, and though her master, for aught she knew, lay expiring in an apoplexy [stroke].

It will not be wondered at that a creature who had so strict a regard to decency in her own person should be shocked at the least deviation from it in another. She therefore no sooner opened the door, and saw her master standing by the bedside in his shirt, with a candle in his hand, than she started back in a most terrible fright.... Sneerers and profane wits may perhaps laugh at her first fright; yet my graver reader, when he considers the time of night, the summons from her bed, and the situation in which she found her master, will highly justify and applaud her conduct, unless the prudence which must be supposed to attend maidens at that period of life at which Mrs. Deborah had arrived, should a little lessen his admiration.

Because Fielding writes from the third-person omniscient point of view, we get a full picture of this scene. We know exactly what both Mr. Allworthy and Mrs. Deborah think: he is astonished and "touched with sentiments of compassion" at the sight of the baby; she doesn't even notice the baby at first because she is so frightened by the sight of her master in an indecent state, wearing just a shirt, without his coat. We know, too, that Fielding wishes us to see Mrs. Deborah as a character very concerned with decency—not only does he show us this when she takes the time to fix her hair before attending to her master's urgent summons, but he also tells us that we should "highly **justify** and applaud her conduct" when we consider the situation she was in. With this intrusion, Fielding reminds us that we are readers (he even calls us such) and that he is in control of the story.

Although the third-person omniscient point of view can keep readers from completely connecting with any one character (you probably noticed that you didn't feel as close to either Mr. Allworthy or Mrs. Deborah as you did to Huck Finn or Peyton Farquhar), it has the benefit of allowing an author to write without limits. In writing a story from the omniscient point of view, you don't have to worry about how your narrator would interpret events or try to work him into scenes that are necessary to the story but at which he would be unlikely to be present.

Just because there are no limits to what you *can* include as an omniscient author, however, doesn't mean there are not limits to what you *should* include. You still want your story to make sense and be easy to follow—and to keep readers interested.

And, these days, you probably want to stay away from authorial intrusion, as most modern readers are likely to be annoyed by an author's interruptions. Even flitting from one character's head to the next throughout the course of a scene may ring false to some readers; because none of us has the ability to be inside anyone's head but our own, a narrator who is in everyone's head at once may seem unbelievable. For this reason, omniscient narrators are not as common as they once were, although they do still appear in some modern literary works. This does not mean that omniscient narration isn't worth an attempt. Many authors consider omniscience one of the hardest viewpoints to write, and if you can master it, you should be able to master any of the more **contemporary** viewpoints!

MANY VOICES,

As authors who write from the omniscient perspective understand, sometimes one point of view just isn't enough to convey the full meaning of a story. In this case, many modern authors turn to the technique of multiple viewpoint. Like omniscience, multiple viewpoint allows authors to tell readers the thoughts of more than one character. Unlike omniscience, however, these thoughts are revealed one character at a time, usually in different scenes or chapters, each of which is written from one first- or third-person narrator's point of view.

Using multiple viewpoints allows you to tell readers about scenes that one of the viewpoint characters may not have been involved in. It also gives you the ability to show both (or all three or more) sides of a conflict. You can even present the same scene from two different points of view—first what a girl thought of her birthday party, then what her brother thought, for example. While this can seem like an interesting and exciting technique, you should use it only if your story absolutely calls for it, and even then, you should create only as many narrators as are necessary to tell the full story. Switching viewpoints among too many characters, or when it is unnecessary to do so, can prevent readers from fully connecting with your characters or can jar them from the illusion of your story.

If you do find that a multiple viewpoint will enhance your story, it's important to think of each narrator as a separate individual and to give each her own voice. Notice how American author Barbara Kingsolver does just that in the following excerpt from *The Poisonwood Bible* (1998). Throughout the novel, Kingsolver writes about a family's missionary journey to Africa from the points of view of four sisters, each narrating a chapter at a time. Following are segments of each sister's opening chapter.

ONE STORY

Leah Price

We stood blinking for a moment, staring out through the dust at a hundred dark villagers,

slender and silent, swaying faintly like trees. We'd left Georgia at the height of a peach-blossom summer and

now stood in a bewildering dry, red fog that seemed like no particular season you could put your finger on. In

all our layers of clothing we must have resembled a family of Eskimos plopped down in a jungle.

But that was our burden, because there was so much we needed to bring here....

Ruth May Price

Our village is going to have this many white people: me, Rachel, Leah, and Adah. Mama. Father.

That is six people. Rachel is oldest, I am youngest. Leah and Adah are in between and they're twins, so maybe

they are one person, but I think two, because Leah runs everywhere and climbs trees, but Adah can't, she is bad

on one whole side and doesn't talk because she is brain-damaged and also hates us all....

Rachel Price

Man oh man, are we in for it now, was my thinking about the Congo from the instant we first set foot. We are supposed to be calling the shots here, but it doesn't look to me like we're in charge of a thing, not even our own selves. Father had planned a big old prayer meeting as a welcome ceremony, to prove that God had ensued us here and aimed to settle in. But when we stepped off the airplane and staggered out into the field with our bags, the Congolese people surrounded us—Lordy!—in a chanting broil. Charmed, I'm sure....

Adah Price

Sunrise tantalize, evil eyes hypnotize: that is the morning, Congo pink. Any

morning, every morning. Blossomy rose-color birdsong air streaked sour with breakfast cookfires.

A wide red plank of dirt—the so-called road—flat-out in front of us, continuous in theory from here to

somewhere distant. But the way I see it through my Adah eyes it is a flat plank clipped into pieces,

rectangles and trapezoids, by the skinny black-line shadows of tall palm trunks.

Even after reading only these short excerpts in each narrator's voice, you could probably pick up this book, open to a random page, and identify which sister was narrating, so successfully has Kingsolver created four completely different narrators. Just as each of the sisters has a unique narrative voice, so also does each look at the world in a different way, giving us different perspectives of the family's life in Africa. Had Kingsolver chosen to write this novel from the viewpoint of only one character, she wouldn't have been able to give us the complete story, not only because there are scenes that don't involve all of the sisters, but also because each experiences her family's journey differently. And, if Kingsolver had chosen to write in the omniscient point of view—in which we could also have learned of each sister's thoughts—we would have lost much of our connection with the narrators, as we would have heard not their voices, but the author's.

One of the reasons that Kingsolver's use of the multiple viewpoint works so well is that she has created four narrators who are equally **compelling**. They all add value to the story. If you choose to write a story with multiple viewpoints, you should strive to achieve the same. Otherwise, your readers may resent being taken out of the viewpoint of their favorite character to follow the life of a narrator for whom they care little.

Also, in order to keep your readers from becoming confused, be sure to indicate whenever you shift viewpoint (usually with a blank line or chapter break), and make sure we know right away whose viewpoint we are in (by labeling the section or referring to the character's name in the first sentence or two). Used successfully, multiple viewpoint can offer readers a rich experience, showing how our individual personalities shape our understanding of the events that surround us. Remember that most stories have at least two sides, and if you try to see both—or all—of them, you may just find yourself writing a page-turner in multiple viewpoint!

CAN WE TRUST HIM?

Usually, when readers pick up a novel or a short story, they automatically believe what the narrator is telling them—not believe it in the sense that they think it really happened, but in the sense that they think the narrator is telling the story in a straightforward manner. Sometimes, though, especially in the first-person, narrators prove to be unreliable. Either because they are naïve or deceitful or deluded, these narrators don't tell the whole truth of the story, or they mistakenly interpret it. In the case of such narrators, readers are left to judge for themselves how much of the story is accurate and how much is skewed—with the help of clues left by the author. Such clues can involve showing an event in which the narrator's interpretation of another's action is clearly wrong or having the narrator admit to lying to readers about one thing—which can lead them to wonder what else he is lying about.

Trying to determine to what extent a narrator is trustworthy can be a difficult task for readers. Some embrace this challenge, as it makes them feel as if they are part of the story, detectives trying to separate fictional truth from lies. Others, however, may quickly give up on a story that seems to be filled with lies or contradictions or is hard to follow. Some may even be angered if the author doesn't make clear in the end how much of the story was true and how much was distorted by the unreliable narrator. Most readers want to find out at some point what "really" happened. But it takes a skillful author to make this clear when telling a tale through the eyes of an unreliable narrator.

As you read the following excerpt from the short story "The Tell-Tale Heart" (1843) by American author Edgar Allan Poe, watch for signs that the first-person narrator, who recounts the tale of a murder he committed, is not reliable. What kinds of clues does Poe provide to help us figure out which parts of the story are true and which aren't?

True!—nervous—very, very dreadfully nervous I had been and am! but why will you say that I am mad? The disease had sharpened my senses—not destroyed—not dulled them. Above all was the sense of hearing acute. I heard all things in the heaven and in the earth. I heard many things in hell. How, then, am I mad? Hearken! and observe how healthily—how calmly I can tell you the whole story.

It is impossible to say how first the idea entered my brain; but once conceived, it haunted me day and night. Object there was none. Passion there was none. I loved the old man. He had never wronged me. He had never given me insult. For his gold I had no desire. I think it was his eye! yes, it was this! He had the eye of a vulture—a pale blue eye, with a film over it. Whenever it fell upon me, my blood ran cold; and so by degrees—very gradually—I made up my mind to take the life of the old man, and thus rid myself of the eye forever.

Now this is the point. You fancy me mad. Madmen know nothing. But you should have seen me. You should have seen how wisely I proceeded—with what caution—with what foresight—with what dissimulation I went to work!

I was never kinder to the old man than during the whole week before I killed him. And every night, about midnight, I turned the latch of his door and opened it—oh, so gently! And then, when I had made an opening sufficient for my head, I put in a dark lantern, all closed, closed, so that no light shone out, and then I thrust in my head. Oh, you would have laughed to see how cunningly I thrust it in! I moved it slowly—very, very slowly, so that I might not disturb the old man's sleep. It took me an hour to place my whole head within the opening so far that I could see him as he lay upon his bed. Ha!—would a madman have been so wise as this?

After reading this excerpt, one thing is clear: despite the narrator's statements to the contrary, he certainly *is* mad. And this is what makes him unreliable. He interprets his actions—including killing a man because of his eye—as those of a sane man. Throughout the text, Poe gives us clues to the narrator's madness: his claim that he heard things in heaven and hell, his calmness as he carried out his murderous plan, and his pride in how "cunningly" he thrust his head in the door. Yet, though he is an unreliable narrator, we are also led to believe that parts of his story are true. For example, he did plan carefully and proceed cautiously, and he did commit the murder. Although Poe's narrator could be lying to us, it seems more likely that he himself doesn't recognize his madness—thus, he is telling us the story as he honestly sees it. In other cases, unreliable narrators may deliberately lie to readers, perhaps trying to get them to condemn another character or see their own actions as justified. In any case, the story—and our interpretation of it—is dramatically altered when it is told by an unreliable narrator.

Experimenting with narrators—reliable or unreliable, first-person or third-person—allows you to experiment with your whole story, subtly or significantly changing its feel, its look, and even its overall meaning. Finding the right point of view means finding the right story, the one that's just waiting to be told—and the person who's waiting to tell it. So try her point of view and his, yours and mine. Eventually, you will find the point of view that pulls the reader off of his chair and into the life of your story!

Edgar Allan Poe (1809–1849)

The best way to learn to write in different viewpoints is to carefully observe the world around you, read works by many different authors, and, most of all, practice. To help get you started, try these exercises.

BE SOMEONE DIFFERENT Think about someone who is not at all like you— maybe someone who is outgoing if you are shy, maybe a football player if you don't play sports. Imagine how he or she sees the world. Then, basing your narrator loosely on this person, write a first-person narrative about his or her first trip to a big city. Remember that although you are writing the word "I," you are not writing about how you would experience the trip, but how this character would. Because we are already in the narrator's head, you don't need to use phrases like "I thought"—just show us what he or she thought. Try to give the narrator a unique voice, choosing words that he or she would use.

A DIFFERENT VIEW Choose a short story or novel written in the third-person limited point of view. Think about how the author's choice of viewpoint character affects the story. Now think about the other characters in the story. Choose one of them and rewrite a scene in the story with this character as the viewpoint character.

Remember that you can now take us inside this character's head, but not inside any-one else's. Don't be afraid to change the story dramatically to reflect this narrator's perceptions. If you retold the story of "Cinderella" from the viewpoint of one of the stepsisters, for example, you would likely end up with a much different story than the one we get from Cinderella's point of view

ANALYZING OMNISCIENCE Pick a novel written from the omniscient point of view, such as Henry Fielding's *Tom Jones* or Jane Austen's *Pride and Prejudice*. Read the book carefully, looking for examples of authorial intrusion. Such intrusion might be as blatant as a paragraph addressing you as "dear reader," or it may be as subtle as a statement about what unmarried men are like. As you read, also try to identify how many characters' thoughts the author reveals—and how often the author takes us into the heads of each of these characters. After you have finished the novel, think about whether or not the omniscient point of view was the best choice to tell the story. How would its effect on you have been different if the book had been written in a more limited viewpoint?

A FAMILY TALE Think about a recent event that involved your whole family in some way. First, write about your own experience of the event: how you were involved, how it made you feel, what changed in your life as a result. Then, try to imagine how the other members of your family experienced the event. Write a separate account of the event from each of their perspectives, using the first-person point of view for each. At the beginning of each section, be sure to make clear who is speaking, and as you write, try to call to mind how each of your family members talks so that you can create a unique voice for each.

LISTENING FOR THE UNRELIABLE The next time a friend tells you a story about something that happened to herself, listen carefully not only to what she is saying, but to how she is saying it. Do you think she is being completely faithful to the details of the story, or do you think she is trying to slant her telling of the story so that you will see her in a more positive light or see things her way? After listening to the story, write a brief summary of it as your friend told it, then write a short analysis of why you think your friend was or wasn't a reliable narrator.

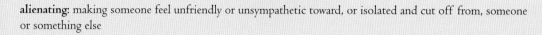

GLOSSARY

alienating: making someone feel unfriendly or unsympathetic toward, or isolated and cut off from, someone or something else

compelling: powerfully attractive and able to hold someone's attention

contemporary: of the present time

exposition: the part of a work of fiction that reveals information about the story's background, setting, or characters

fictional: not real; part of an imaginary story

first person: a perspective, pronoun, or verb form that refers to the speaker or writer; in English, "I," "we," and "us" are first-person pronouns

justify: find acceptable

omniscient: all-knowing, with unlimited understanding and insight

peripheral: on the outer edge; a peripheral character is a minor character who is not at the center of a story

perspective: the position from which a person views people, objects, or events; how a person sees the world

prose: speech or writing that is not poetry, but sounds more like everyday speech

protagonist: the main character in a work of fiction

scenes: single episodes in short stories or novels

style: the way in which an author writes, as distinct from what he or she writes

third person: a perspective, pronoun, or verb form that refers to someone or something being spoken about; in English, third-person pronouns include "he," "she," "it," and "they"

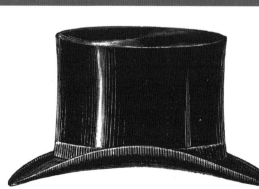

BIBLIOGRAPHY

Booth, Wayne C. *The Rhetoric of Fiction*. Chicago: University of Chicago Press, 1983.

Card, Orson Scott. *Characters and Viewpoint*. Cincinnati, Ohio: Writer's Digest Books, 1988.

DeMarinis, Rick. *The Art & Craft of the Short Story*. Cincinnati, Ohio: Story Press, 2000.

Kress, Nancy. *Characters, Emotion & Viewpoint*. Cincinnati, Ohio: Writer's Digest Books, 2005.

Rubie, Peter. *The Elements of Storytelling*. New York: John Wiley & Sons, 1996.

Stevick, Philip. *The Theory of the Novel*. New York: The Free Press, 1967.

Szeman, Sherri. *Mastering Point of View*. Cincinnati, Ohio: Story Press, 2001.

FURTHER READING

Bierce, Ambrose. *The Complete Short Stories of Ambrose Bierce*. Compiled by Ernest Jerome Hopkins. Lincoln: University of Nebraska Press, 1985.

Fielding, Henry. *The History of Tom Jones, a Foundling*. New York: The Heritage Press, 1952.

Kingsolver, Barbara. *The Poisonwood Bible*. New York: HarperTorch, 1998.

Poe, Edgar Allan. *The Complete Tales and Poems of Edgar Allan Poe*. Compiled by Edward H. O'Neill. New York: Dorset Press, 1989.

Twain, Mark. *The Adventures of Huckleberry Finn*. New York: Random House, 1996.

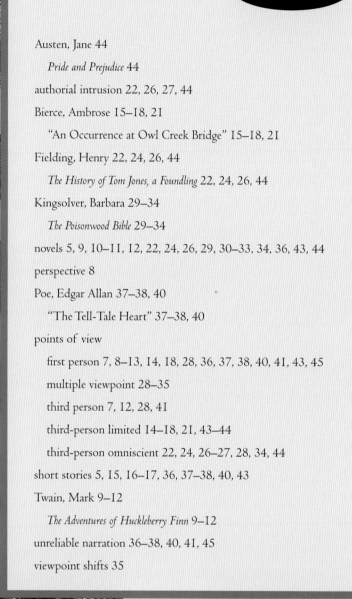

INDEX